Zip, Whiz, Zoom!

Zip, Whiz, Zoom!

Stephanie Calmenson

Pictures by Dorothy Stott

Little, Brown and Company
Boston Toronto London

First Edition

Library of Congress Cataloging-in-Publication Data

Calmenson, Stephanie.
    Zip, whiz, zoom! / by Stephanie Calmenson; pictures by Dorothy
Stott.   — 1st ed.
        p.   cm.
    ISBN 0-316-12478-8
    1. Transportation— Juvenile literature. [1. Transportation.]
I. Stott, Dorothy, ill.   II. Title.
TA1149.C35   1992
629.04—dc20   90-40885

Joy Street Books are published by Little, Brown and Company (Inc.)
10 9 8 7 6 5 4 3 2 1
WOR
Published simultaneously in Canada by
Little, Brown & Company (Canada) Limited
Printed in the United States of America

To Nathan and Rachel Mittag
— S. C.

To Robert Lewis Burdick,
my first and dearest Vermont friend,
who made it possible for me to finish
these wonderful paintings
— D. S.

ZIP, WHIZ, ZOOM!
We're on our way!
We're going somewhere
special today.

ZIP onto the airplane.
It's waiting at the gate.
We made it in the nick of time.
Today we can't be late.

WHIZ through the tunnel.
This train is moving fast!
We wave out the window
At the people we go past.

ZOOM down the highway.
On the bus we play a game —
Counting all the cars we see
That look almost the same.

HONK! Traffic tie-up!
A taxi just broke down.
Please tow it quickly.
We are going out of town.

WHIRR! You can hear us.
You can see us as we rise.
Feel the wind that's blowing
When our helicopter flies.

VROOM! Hear the motor
As we bounce along the road.
We know our truck will make it
Even with this heavy load.

TOOT-TOOT! Our ferry boat
Sails across the bay.
We feed the hungry birds
That we meet along the way.

BEEP-BEEP! Bicycles!
Go up the hills and down.
Pedal, pedal faster!
Soon we'll reach the town.

BOOM-DE-BOOM! Beat the drums!
Play a happy tune!
Here we come! We're on our way!
We'll all be there by noon.

Hurry, hurry to the door.
Finally we are there . . .
We came all the way to Grandma's house
By land and sea and air!

RAILROAD
STATION

We came for Grandma's birthday.
It's a very special day.
When she asks us how we got here,
This is what we say . . .